READINGS FOR YOUR WEDDING

Edited by Brian Magee CM

VERITAS

First published 1985 by
Veritas Publications
7/8 Lower Abbey Street
Dublin 1

Second edition published 1995
Reprinted 2009

ISBN 978 1 85390 253 6

Cover design: Lir Mac Cárthaigh
Printed in the Republic of Ireland by ColourBooks Ltd, Dublin

Veritas books are printed on paper made from the wood pulp of managed forests. For every tree felled, at least one tree is planted, thereby renewing natural resources.

CONTENTS

Gospel Readings

**Additions to the 1990 edition of the Marriage Rite (2nd Editio Typica)*

INTRODUCTION

The Role of the Reader

To be asked to read at the Wedding Mass is indeed a compliment and a privilege. You are seen as a friend and helper of the couple being married and their families. It presumes that you have the ability to read, to speak clearly and to speak out.

But there is more to the task than that. The couple have chosen the readings for this Mass. These texts speak to them of the meaning of their love and marriage, so it is important for them that they be read well. The congregation at the Mass will be interested in what is being said about this marriage and also in what is being said about their own marriages and lives.

The texts will be familiar enough, but new light will always be thrown on them by the circumstances in which they are heard. The preacher will try to bring out the comfort and encouragement, the strengthening and warning they contain. It is up to the reader to make sure that the readings are heard and understood. Preparation is needed, and not just for pronunciation and grammar. The preparation must be a prayerful one, searching out what the Holy Spirit, who is alive and active in the inspired Word of God, is saying. It means finding some background information on what the reading is saying, and that can come from books or from someone who is knowledgeable about Scripture. Ideally, the message should, through study and prayer, become part of the reader, through whom the dead words in the book become alive for the congregation.

The Texts that are Read

The Wedding Mass readings have been chosen not only because they have something human and beatiful to say about love and marriage, but mainly because they express the Christian understanding of marriage. A Christian wedding is a celebration of the Sacrament of Matrimony. Words and actions come together to express the deepest meanings of marriage.

In the first part of the Mass, before the vows are made, we listen to the Word of God. Scripture readings are taken from the Mass Lectionary, and in this book we deal only with the section especially prepared for weddings. We include five extra readings added in recent years. These are placed after the ones in the original Lectionary. For a clearer understanding we have used the *New Revised Standard Version* and *New Jerusalem* translations. The church lectionary may have a different version.

The choice of texts will be made with the couple. Some thought and prayer should go into the particular choices in order to appreciate their meaning. For this reason the Gospel passages are also included here so that the couple and the priest may choose an appropriate one, and perhaps talk about what will be said in the homily. The reader's task will be to ensure that the couple's understanding of these texts is brought out for the congregation.

Sometimes the couples have favourite passages from poets and philosophers that speak to them about their love. These can never be a substitute for the Word of God but may be used as commentaries, as meditations, or as illustrations in the homily.

How to Prepare

The texts are generally quite short. This is a help if you

are nervous, but it does mean that you have to make sure the message gets across to people who are actively listening. First, make sure that you have no problems with pronunciation. Read the text out loud to get the feel of the sentences. Remember that you will tend to read too fast, so learn to pause and control your speed. See what the main point of the reading is. The small sentence in italics at the beginning is the main sentence of the reading. This small sentence is only a help and should not be read out loud. It may help to know where the passage comes from in the Bible, what the original circumstances of the message were. Further help may come from knowing which aspect of Christian marriage the text speaks about, and how the priest will use it in his homily. Best of all, if you can come to like the reading and feel that it speaks to you, then you can enjoy telling others about it. That is what preaching the Gospel is about. For we know that when the scriptures are read in the church, God himself speaks to his people. The reader shares in the work of spreading the good news of Jesus Christ. The Wedding Mass can be one of those occasions when people are especially attentive. The reader should be ready to fulfil their expectations.

A word about the Responsorial Psalm. Normally this will be sung, but if it is to be read, remember that it is a poem and has a musical rhythm. An introduction is supplied here for each psalm to help people to understand what the prayer is about. The reader should help the congregation to remember the psalm by repeating the antiphon or response with them, but should never cue them in by saying: 'Response!'

Prayer of the Faithful

Sometimes, as well as having to read them, readers are involved in the preparation of intentions for the Prayer of the Faithful. This will help their reading preparation.

Here are some points to remember. These are general intentions; we pray for the whole Church, for the whole world that is in need of salvation, for the local community and its needs, and for the couple, who have just been married. Normally there are about five intentions, and on the occasion of a wedding they will centre on the idea of marriage, e.g. asking help for all married couples, for the protection of this marriage, for others preparing for marriage, for deceased relatives of the couple or for those who are absent on this happy occasion.

It is important to remember that the reader is talking to the congregation, suggesting intentions that the congregation is to pray for. The reader is not praying but is asking others to pray. So the usual form will begin with 'Let us pray for' or, 'Let us ask the Lord in prayer for', or some such expression. It is the gathered congregation which petitions with and through Christ. These intentions should not be rushed – allow people time to think about them and pray. If the prayer response of the congregation can be sung so much the better. The example and help of Mary can be included in the expression of intentions, but the saying of the Hail Mary has no place in the Prayer of the Faithful. An example of a complete set of intentions is given in the *Wedding Ritual and People's Book* (Veritas).

Points to Remember

Never read unprepared.

Understand what you read.

Slow down! You read faster than you think you do.

Don't start too soon. Wait until everyone is ready.

Pause before you say 'This is the word of the Lord'.

Take your time walking up to and down from the lectern.

Know, love and care about the Scripture.

Speak the text out loud in preparation.

Don't accept an invitation to read all the readings, one is work enough.

Check the Lectionary and the microphone beforehand.

Always read from the Lectionary, not from a piece of paper.

Look at the congregation to catch their attention.

Vary your pace, mood, inflection and projection.

Remember, the psalm is a poem.

Do not say 'response' after each stanza.

Pray that you may hear the Word of God and keep it.

Talk to the congregation, not the microphone.

Remember to speak slowly but not softly.

If you cannot be heard, the Word of God cannot be heard.

What is communicated is not what is said but what is heard.

Be very clear on when exactly you have to come forward to read.

Don't rush! Give the congregation time to reflect on each theme.

OLD TESTAMENT READINGS

Reading 1

This reading speaks to us about God's love and care for man and woman in their relationship with each other. Human love and sexuality are seen as good and blessed by God. And it reminds us that God does not create and then forget his creation, but that his love and protection will be with this couple all their married life. The three poetic lines in the middle of the passage will need special attention from the reader.

NRSV

A reading from the book of Genesis *1:26-28.31*

Male and female he created them.

God said, 'Let us make humankind in our image, according to our likeness; and let them have dominion over the fish of the sea, and over the birds of the air, and over the cattle, and over all the wild animals of the earth, and over every creeping thing that creeps upon the earth.'

So God created humankind in his image,
in the image of God he created them;
male and female he created them.

God blessed them, and God said to them, 'Be fruitful and multiply, and fill the earth and subdue it; and have dominion over the fish of the sea and over the birds of the air and over every living thing that moves upon the earth.' God saw everything that he had made, and indeed, it was very good.

This is the word of the Lord.

NJB

A reading from the book of Genesis *1:26-28.31*

Male and female he created them.

God said, 'Let us make man in our own image, in the likeness of ourselves, and let them be masters of the fish of the sea, the birds of heaven, the cattle, all the wild animals and all the creatures that creep along the ground.'

God created man in the image of himself,
in the image of God he created him,
male and female he created them.

God blessed them, saying to them, 'Be fruitful, multiply, fill the earth and subdue it. Be masters of the fish of the sea, the birds of heaven, and all the living creatures that move on earth.'
God saw all he had made, and indeed it was very good.

This is the word of the Lord.

Pronunciation: GENesis

Responsorial Psalm 1 *Ps 32:12.18.20-22. R v.5*

If the Responsorial Psalm is not sung the following introduction may be used:

God's love and care are seen in all the works of creation, and in human love. We can indeed respond to the Psalm saying:

℟ The Lord fills the earth with his love.

1. They are happy, whose God is the Lord,
the people he has chosen as his own.
The Lord looks on those who revere him,
on those who hope in his love. ℟

2. Our soul is waiting for the Lord.
The Lord is our help and our shield.
In him do our hearts find joy.
We trust in his holy name. ℟

3. May your love be upon us, O Lord,
as we place all our hope in you. ℟

Reading 2

The writer of this passage is not teaching history, but is exploring God's creation. The need for companionship is understood by God. Man and woman complement each other, they are each individuals but fulfil each other's needs. They are equal but different.

NRSV

A reading from the book of Genesis *2:18-24*

They become one flesh.

The Lord God said, 'It is not good that the man should be alone; I will make him a helper as his partner.' So out of the ground the Lord God formed every animal of the field and every bird of the air, and brought them to the man to see what he would call them; and whatever the man called every living creature, that was its name. The man gave names to all cattle, and to the birds of the air, and to every animal of the field; but for the man there was not found a helper as his partner. So the Lord God caused a deep sleep to fall upon the man, and he slept; then he took one of his ribs and closed up its place with flesh. And the rib that the Lord God had taken from the man he made into a woman and brought her to the man. Then the man said, 'This at last is bone of my bones and flesh of my flesh; this one shall be called Woman, for out of Man this one was taken.' Therefore a man leaves his father and his mother and clings to his wife, and they become one flesh.

This is the word of the Lord.

NJB

A reading from the book of Genesis *2:18-24*

They become one flesh.

The Lord God said, 'It is not right that the man should be alone. I shall make him a helper. So from the soil the Lord God fashioned all the wild animals and all the birds of heaven. These he brought to the man to see what he would call them; each one was to bear the name the man would give it. The man gave names to all the cattle, all the birds of heaven and all the wild animals. But no helper suitable for the man was found for him. Then, the Lord God made the man fall into a deep sleep. And, while he was asleep, he took one of his ribs and closed the flesh up again forthwith. The Lord God fashioned the rib he had taken from the man into a woman, and brought her to the man. And the man said:

This one at last is bone of my bones
 and flesh of my flesh!
She is to be called Woman,
 because she was taken from Man.

This is why a man leaves his father and mother and becomes attached to his wife, and they become one flesh.

This is the word of the Lord.

Responsorial Psalm 2 *Ps 148:1-4.9-14.R v.12* **Psalm 2**

If the Responsorial Psalm is not sung the following introduction may be used:

When we look at the marvellous ways of God in his creation we are led to respond:

℟ Praise the name of the Lord.
or
℟ Alleluia!

1 Praise the Lord from the heavens,
praise him in the heights.
Praise him, all his angels,
praise him, all his host. ℟

2 Praise him, sun and moon,
praise him, shining stars.
Praise him, highest heavens
and the waters above the heavens. ℟

3 All mountains and hills,
all fruit trees and cedars,
beasts, wild and tame,
reptiles and birds on the wing. ℟

4 All earth's kings and peoples,
earth's princes and rulers:
young men and maidens,
old men together with children. ℟

5 Let them praise the name of the Lord
for he alone is exalted.
The splendour of his name
reaches beyond heaven and earth. ℟

Old Testament 3

Reading 3

The biblical story of the marriage of Isaac and Rebekah looks at the mysterious way in which two people come together and at how God's guidance is seen in that meeting. Both Isaac and Rebekah suffer in parting from their families, but their mutual love supports them. Together they must make their own life, being a support to each other in times of difficulty.

NRSV

A reading from the book of Genesis *24:48-51.58-67*

Isaac took Rebekah, and he loved her. So he was comforted after his mother's death.

Abraham's servant said to Laban, 'Then I bowed my head and worshipped the Lord, and blessed the Lord, the God of my master Abraham, who had led me by the right way to obtain the daughter of my master's kinsman for his son. Now then, if you will deal loyally and truly with my master, tell me; and if not, tell me, so that I may turn either to the right hand or to the left.' Then Laban and Bethuel answered, 'The thing comes from the Lord; we cannot speak to you anything bad or good. Look, Rebekah is before you, take her and go, and let her be the wife of your master's son, as the Lord has spoken.' And they called Rebekah, and said to her, 'Will you go with this man?' She said, 'I will.' So they sent away their sister Rebekah and her nurse along with Abraham's servant and his men. And they blessed Rebekah and said to her, 'May you, our sister, become thousands of myriads; may your offspring gain possession of the gates of their foes.' Then Rebekah and her maids rose up, mounted the camels, and followed the man; thus the servant took Rebekah, and went his way. Now Isaac had come from

Beer-lahai-roi, and was settled in the Negeb. Isaac went out in the evening to walk in the field; and looking up, he saw camels coming. And Rebekah looked up, and when she saw Isaac, she slipped quickly from the camel, and said to the servant, 'Who is the man over there, walking in the field to meet us?' The servant said, 'It is my master.' So she took her veil and covered herself. And the servant told Isaac all the things that he had done. Then Isaac brought her into his mother Sarah's tent. He took Rebekah, and she became his wife; and he loved her. So Isaac was comforted after his mother's death.

This is the word of the Lord.

NJB

A reading from the book of Genesis *24:48-51.58-67*

In his love for Rebekah, Isaac was consoled for the loss of his mother.

Abraham's servant said to Laban, 'Then I bowed down and worshipped the Lord, and I blessed the Lord, God of my master Abraham, who had led me by a direct path to choose the daughter of my master's brother for his son. Now tell me whether you are prepared to show constant and faithful love to my master; if not, say so, and I shall know what to do.'

Laban and Bethuel replied, 'This is from the Lord; it is not for us to say yes or no to you. Rebekah is there before you. Take her and go; and let her become the wife of your master's son, as the Lord has decreed.' They called Rebekah and asked her, 'Will you go with this man?' She replied, 'I will.' Accordingly they let their sister Rebekah go, with her nurse, and Abraham's servant and his men. They blessed Rebekah and said to her:

Sister of ours, from you may there spring
thousands and tens of thousands!
May your descendants gain possession
of the gates of their enemies!

And forthwith, Rebekah and her maids mounted the camels, and followed the man. The servant took Rebekah and departed.

Isaac meanwhile had come back from the well of Lahai Roi and was living in the Negeb. While Isaac was out walking towards evening in the fields, he looked up and saw camels approaching. And Rebekah looked up and saw Isaac. She jumped down from her camel, and asked the servant, 'Who is that man walking through the fields towards us?' The servant replied, 'That is my master.' So she took her veil and covered herself up. The servant told Isaac the whole story. Then Isaac took her into his tent. He married Rebekah and made her his wife. And in his love for her, Isaac was consoled for the loss of his mother.

This is the word of the Lord.

Pronunciation:
Abraham (a as in bay)
RebEKah
LABan (a as in bay)
I-saac (i as in bite)
BETHuel
NEgeb
LaHa-i Ro-i

Responsorial Psalm 3 *Ps 144:8-10.15.17-18. R v.9*

If the Responsorial Psalm is not sung the following introduction may be used:

The power of God is seen in the marriage of Isaac and Rebekah. He protects all who trust in him; in our response to the psalm we thank him for that care:

℟ How good is the Lord to all.

1 The Lord is kind and full of compassion,
slow to anger, abounding in love.
How good is the Lord to all,
compassionate to all his creatures. ℟

2 All your creatures shall thank you, O Lord,
and your friends shall repeat their blessing.
The eyes of all creatures look to you
and you give them their food in due time. ℟

3 The Lord is just in all his ways
and loving in all his deeds.
He is close to all who call him,
who call on him from their hearts. ℟

Reading 4

The message here is that even in Old Testament times marriage was seen as part of God's plan and blessed by him and was regulated by the laws of the Covenant. The grace and peace of God go with a marriage celebrated in such faith. The reader will notice some difficulties. The terms 'brother' and 'sister' are used in the broader sense of relatives or even of husband and wife. And notice that as Tobias doesn't know the angel Raphael's true identity he calls him by his assumed name of Azarias.

NRSV

A reading from the book of Tobit *7:6-14*

May the Lord of heaven, my child, guide and prosper you and grant you mercy and peace.

Raguel jumped up and kissed Tobias and wept. He also spoke to him as follows, 'Blessings on you, my child, son of a good and noble father!' 'O most miserable of calamities that such an upright and beneficent man has become blind!' He then embraced his kinsman Tobias and wept. His wife Edna also wept for him, and their daughter Sarah likewise wept. Then Raguel slaughtered a ram from the flock and received them very warmly. When they had bathed and washed themselves and had reclined to dine, Tobias said to Raphael, 'Brother Azariah, ask Raguel to give me my kinswoman Sarah.' But Raguel overheard it and said to the lad, 'Eat and drink, and be merry tonight. For no one except you, brother, has the right to marry my daughter Sarah. Likewise I am not at liberty to give her to any other man than yourself, because you are my nearest relative. But let me explain to you the true situation more fully, my child. I have given her to seven men of our kinsmen, and all died on the night when they went in to her. But now, my child, eat and drink, and the Lord will act on behalf of you both.' But Tobias said, 'I will neither eat nor drink anything until you settle the things that pertain to me.' So Raguel said, 'I will do so. She is given to you in accordance with the decree in the book of Moses, and it has been decreed from heaven that she be given to you. Take your kinswoman; from now on you are her brother and she is your sister. She is given to you from today and forever. May the Lord of heaven, my child, guide and prosper you both this night and grant you mercy and peace.' Then Raguel summoned his daughter Sarah. When she came to him he took her by the hand and gave her to Tobias, saying, 'Take her to be your wife in accordance with the law and decree written in the book of Moses. Take her and bring her safely to your father. And may the God of heaven prosper your journey with his peace.' Then he called her mother and told her to bring writing material; and he wrote out a copy of a marriage contract, to the effect that he gave her to him as wife according to the decree of the law of Moses.

Then they began to eat and drink.

This is the word of the Lord.

NJB

A reading from the book of Tobit *7:6-14*

The Lord of heaven favour you and grant you his grace and peace.

Raguel said to Tobias, 'Blessings on you, child! You are the son of a noble father. How sad it is that someone so bright and full of good deeds should have gone blind!' He fell on the neck of his kinsman Tobias and wept. And his wife Edna wept for him, and so did his daughter Sarah. Raguel killed a ram from his flock, and they gave him a warm welcome.

They washed and bathed and sat down to table. Then Tobias said to Raphael, 'Brother Azarias, will you ask Raguel to give me my sister Sarah?' Raguel overheard the words, and said to the young man, 'Eat and drink, and make the most of your evening; no one else has the right to take my daughter Sarah – no one but you, my brother. In any case even I am not at liberty to give her to anyone else, since you are her next of kin. However, my boy, I must be frank with you: I have tried to find a husband for her seven times among our kinsmen, and all of them have died the first evening, on going to her room. But for the present, my boy, eat and drink; the Lord will grant you his grace and peace.' Tobias spoke out, 'I will not hear of eating and drinking till you have come to a decision about me.' Raguel answered, 'Very well. Since, by the prescription of the Book of Moses she is given to you, Heaven itself decrees she shall be yours. I therefore entrust your sister to you. From now on you are her brother and she is your sister. She is given to you from today for ever. The Lord of heaven favour you tonight, my child, and grant you his grace and peace.' Raguel called for his daughter Sarah, took her by the hand and gave her to Tobias with these words, 'I entrust her to you; the law and the ruling recorded in the Book of Moses assign her to you as your wife. Take her; bring her home safe and sound to your father's house. The God of heaven grant you a good journey in peace.' Then he turned to her mother and asked her to fetch him writing paper. He drew up the marriage contract, and so he gave his daughter as bride to Tobias according to the ordinance of the Law of Moses.

After this they began to eat and drink.

This is the word of the Lord.

Pronunciation:
TObit
Ragu-el
ToBIas (i as in bite)
RAPHa-el (a as in bay)

Responsorial Psalm 4 *Ps 32:12.18.20-22. R v.5*

If the Responsorial Psalm is not sung the following introduction may be used:

Grace and peace come to all who live according to God's law; his love goes with them as we acclaim in the response to the Psalm:

℟ The Lord fills the earth with his love.

1 They are happy, whose God is the Lord,
the people he has chosen as his own.
The Lord looks on those who revere him,
on those who hope in his love. ℟

2 Our soul is waiting for the Lord.
The Lord is our help and our shield.
In him do our hearts find joy.
We trust in his holy name. ℟

3 May your love be upon us, O Lord,
as we place all our hope in you. ℟

Reading 5

Right from the beginning of their marriage Tobias and Sarah prayed together. Praying together is a deep level of sharing, and prayer in the family will be a source of bonding. The reader should try to bring out the two parts of this reading, the narrative account and the actual prayer. The prayer should be read at a speed which allows reflection on the meaning.

NRSV

A reading from the book of Tobit *8:4-8*

Grant that we may grow old together.

On the evening of their marriage, Tobias said to Sarah, 'Let us pray and implore our Lord that he grant us mercy and safety.' Tobias began by saying,
'Blessed are you, O God of our ancestors,
and blessed is your name
in all generations forever.
Let the heavens and the whole creation
bless you forever.
You made Adam,
and for him you made his wife Eve
as a helper and support.
From the two of them the human race has sprung.
You said,
"It is not good that the man should be alone;
let us make a helper for him like himself."
I now am taking this kinswoman of mine,
not because of lust,
but with sincerity.
Grant that she and I may find mercy
and that we may grow old together.'
And they both said, 'Amen, Amen.'

This is the word of the Lord.

NJB

A reading from the book of Tobit *8:4-8*

Bring us to old age together.

On the evening of their marriage, Tobias said to Sarah, 'You and I must pray and petition our Lord to win his grace and protection.' She stood up, and they began praying for protection, and this was how he began:

> You are blessed, O God of our fathers;
> blessed too is your name
> for ever and ever.
> Let the heavens bless you
> and all things you have made
> for evermore.
>
> You it was who created Adam,
> you who created Eve his wife
> to be his help and support;
> and from these two the human race was born.
> You it was who said,
> 'It is not right that the man should be alone;
> let us make him a helper like him.'
> And so I take my sister
> not from any lustful motive,
> but I do it in singleness of heart.
> Be kind enough to have pity on her and on me
> and bring us to old age together.

And together they said, 'Amen, Amen.'

This is the word of the Lord.

Pronunciation:
TOBit (o as in bone)
ToBIas (i as in bite)

Responsorial Psalm 5

Ps 102:1-2.8.13.17-18. R v.8 Alt. R v.17

Respect for the laws of God is our response to the love that he shows us first; we acknowledge his love in our response:

℟ The Lord is compassion and love.
or
℟ The love of the Lord is everlasting upon those who hold him in fear.

1 My soul, give thanks to the Lord,
all my being, bless his holy name.
My soul, give thanks to the Lord
and never forget all his blessings. ℟

2 The Lord is compassion and love,
slow to anger and rich in mercy.
As a father has compassion on his sons,
the Lord has pity on those who fear him. ℟

3 The love of the Lord is everlasting
upon those who hold him in fear;
his justice reaches out to children's children
when they keep his covenant in truth. ℟

Old Testament 6

Reading 6

This reading is an extract from one of the great love poems of literature. It has its place in the Bible because the relationship of God with his people was seen as one long love match. The language and imagery are those of love poetry. A reader who finds the first verses a bit much could start at 'My beloved speaks and says to me…' / 'My love lifts up his voice…'. The whole passage reminds the couple that their love is for ever.

NRSV

A reading from the Song of Songs *2:8-10.14.16; 8:6-7*

Love is strong as death

The voice of my beloved!
Look, he comes,
leaping upon the mountains,
bounding over the hills.
My beloved is like a gazelle
or a young stag.

Look, there he stands behind our wall,
gazing in at the windows,
looking through the lattice.
My beloved speaks and says to me:
'Arise, my love, my fair one,
and come away;
O my dove, in the clefts of the rock,
in the covert of the cliff,
let me see your face,
let me hear your voice;
for your voice is sweet,
and your face is lovely.'

My beloved is mine and I am his.

Set me as a seal upon your heart,
as a seal upon your arm;
for love is strong as death,
passion fierce as the grave.
Its flashes are flashes of fire,
a raging flame.
Many waters cannot quench love,
neither can floods drown it.

This is the word of the Lord.

NJB

A reading from the Song of Songs *2:8-10.14.16; 8:6-7*

Love is strong as Death.

I hear my love.
See how he comes
leaping on the mountains,
bounding over the hills.
My love is like a gazelle,
like a young stag.

See where he stands
behind our wall.
He looks in at the window,
he peers through the opening.

My love lifts up his voice,
he says to me,
'Come then, my beloved,
my lovely one, come.

My dove, hiding in the clefts of the rock,
in the coverts of the cliff,
show me your face,

let me hear your voice;
for your voice is sweet
and your face is lovely.'
My love is mine and I am his.

Set me like a seal on your heart,
like a seal on your arm.
For love is strong as Death,
passion as relentless as Sheol.
The flash of it is a flash of fire,
a flame of the Lord himself.
Love no flood can quench,
no torrents drown.

This is the word of the Lord.

Pronunciation:
SheOL (o as in old)

Responsorial Psalm 6 *Ps 127:1-5. R cf. v.1*

If the Responsorial Psalm is not sung the following introduction may be used:

The blessings of a united family life are praised in this psalm; our response thanks God for such happiness:

℟ O blessed are those who fear the Lord!

1 O blessed are those who fear the Lord
and walk in his ways!
By the labour of your hands you shall eat.
You will be happy and prosper. ℟

2 Your wife will be like a fruitful vine
in the heart of your house;
your children like shoots of the olive,
around your table. ℟

3 Indeed thus shall be blessed
the man who fears the Lord.
May the Lord bless you from Zion
all the days of your life. ℟

Reading 7

While this reading might seem to put the woman firmly in subjection to her husband, it should be seen in a more positive light. Here the husband lists the positive qualities of the woman he loves. No doubt a wife can make as long a list of the qualities she loves in her husband. Neither loses individuality or independence when each respects and trusts the other.

NRSV

A reading from the book of Sirach *26:1-4.13-16*

Like the sun rising is the beauty of a good wife in her well-ordered home.

Happy is the husband of a good wife;
the number of his days will be doubled.
A loyal wife brings joy to her husband,
and he will complete his years in peace.
A good wife is a great blessing;
she will be granted among the blessings
    of the man who fears the Lord.
Whether rich or poor, his heart is content,
and at all times his face is cheerful.
A wife's charm delights her husband,
and her skill puts flesh on his bones.
A silent wife is a gift from the Lord,
and nothing is so precious as her self-discipline.
A modest wife adds charm to charm,
and no scales can weigh the value of her chastity.
Like the sun rising in the heights of the Lord,
so is the beauty of a good wife in her
    well-ordered home.

This is the word of the Lord.

NJB

A reading from the book of Ecclesiasticus *26:1-4.13-16*

Like the sun rising is the beauty of a good wife in a well-run house.

How blessed is the husband of a really good wife;
the number of his days will be doubled.
A perfect wife is the joy of her husband,
he will live out the years of his life in peace.
A good wife is the best of portions,
reserved for those who fear the Lord;
rich or poor, their hearts will be glad,
their faces cheerful, whatever the season.
The grace of a wife will charm her husband,
her understanding will make him the stronger.
A silent wife is a gift from the Lord,
no price can be put on a well-trained character.
A modest wife is a boon twice over,
a chaste character cannot be over-valued.
Like the sun rising over the mountains of the Lord,
such is the beauty of a good wife in a well-run house.

This is the word of the Lord.

Pronunciation:
EccLESiAsticus (e as in bee)

If the Responsorial Psalm is not sung the following introduction may be used:

Each partner in marriage takes the other for richer, for poorer; but if the Lord is with their union they are always rich; our response prays for the presence of God in this marriage:

℟ I will bless the Lord at all times.
or
℟ Taste and see that the Lord is good.

1 I will bless the Lord at all times,
his praise always on my lips;
in the Lord my soul shall make its boast.
The humble shall hear and be glad. ℟

2 Glorify the Lord with me.
Together let us praise his name.
I sought the Lord and he answered me;
from all my terrors he set me free. ℟

3 Look towards him and be radiant;
let your faces not be abashed.
This poor man called; the Lord heard him
and rescued him from all his distress. ℟

4 The angel of the Lord is encamped
around those who revere him, to rescue them.
Taste and see that the Lord is good.
He is happy who seeks refuge in him. ℟

Old Testament 8

Reading 8

The sacred covenant that God made with his people through Moses laid great stress on the observance of law. The new covenant realised in Jesus Christ is based on the heart, on love. The couple who enter Christian marriage do so through love; their relationship is not a mere business contract, but, rather, a total giving in love.

NRSV

A reading from the prophet Jeremiah *31:31-34*

I will make a new covenant with the house of Israel and the house of Judah.

The days are surely coming, says the Lord, when I will make a new covenant with the house of Israel and the house of Judah. It will not be like the covenant that I made with their ancestors when I took them by the hand to bring them out of the land of Egypt – a covenant that they broke, though I was their husband, says the Lord. But this is the covenant that I will make with the house of Israel after those days, says the Lord: I will put my law within them, and I will write it on their hearts; and I will be their God, and they shall be my people. No longer shall they teach one another, or say to each other, 'Know the Lord,' for they shall all know me, from the least of them to the greatest, says the Lord; for I will forgive their iniquity, and remember their sin no more.

This is the word of the Lord

NJB

A reading from the prophet Jeremiah *31:31-34*

I shall make a new covenant with the House of Israel.

'Look, the days are coming, the Lord declares, when I shall make a new covenant with the House of Israel (and the House of Judah), but not like the covenant I made with their ancestors the day I took them by the hand to bring them out of Egypt, a covenant which they broke, even though I was their Master, the Lord declares. No, this is the covenant I shall make with the House of Israel when those days have come, the Lord declares. Within them I shall plant my Law, writing it on their hearts. Then I shall be their God and they will be my people. There will be no further need for everyone to teach neighbour or brother, saying "Learn to know the Lord!" No, they will all know me, from the least to the greatest, the Lord declares, since I shall forgive their guilt and never more call their sin to mind.'

This is the word of the Lord

Pronunciation:
JeremIah (i as in bite)
ISra-el (a as in bay)
JUDah (u as in Luke)

If the Responsorial Psalm is not sung the following introduction may be used:

Peace and contentment come to those who live with a good conscience, who live according to the will of God. The message of this psalm is summed up in our response:

℟ Happy the man who takes delight in the Lord's commands.

or

℟ Alleluia!

1 Happy the man who fears the Lord,
who takes delight in his commands.
His sons will be powerful on earth;
the children of the upright are blessed. ℟

2 Riches and wealth are in his house;
his justice stands firm forever.
He is a light in the darkness for the upright:
he is generous, merciful and just. ℟

3 The good man takes pity and lends,
he conducts his affairs with honour.
The just man will never waver:
he will be remembered for ever. ℟

4 He has no fear of evil news;
with a firm heart he trusts in the Lord.
With a steadfast heart he will not fear;
he will see the downfall of his foes. ℟

5 Open-handed, he gives to the poor;
his justice stands firm forever.
His head will be raised in glory. ℟

Reading 9

Eastertime is one long festival of celebration. It celebrates the new covenant of Christ with his Church. This reading describes that covenant as a marriage relationship celebrated in an eternal wedding feast. Every Christian marriage reflects that union of Christ with us. Our joy today helps us to understand better the rejoicing in heaven. It is appropriate to use this reading in the Easter Season.

NRSV

A reading from the book of Revelation *19:1.5-9*

Blessed are those who are invited to the marriage supper of the Lamb.

I, John, heard what seemed to be the loud voice of a great multitude in heaven, saying, 'Hallelujah! Salvation and glory and power to our God.'

And from the throne came a voice saying, 'Praise our God, all you his servants, and all who fear him, small and great.' Then I heard what seemed to be the voice of a great multitude, like the sound of many waters and like the sound of mighty thunderpeals, crying out, 'Hallelujah! For the Lord our God the Almighty reigns. Let us rejoice and exult and give him the glory, for the marriage of the Lamb has come, and his bride has made herself ready; to her it has been granted to be clothed with fine linen, bright and pure' – for the fine linen is the righteous deeds of the saints. And the angel said to me, 'Write this: Blessed are those who are invited to the marriage supper of the Lamb.'

This is the word of the Lord.

NJB

A reading from the book of Revelation *19:1.5-9*

Blessed are those who are invited to the wedding feast of the Lamb.

I, John, heard what seemed to be the great sound of a huge crowd in heaven, singing, 'Alleluia! Salvation and glory and power to our God!'

Then a voice came from the throne; it said, 'Praise our God, you servants of his and those who fear him, small and great alike.' And I heard what seemed to be the voices of a huge crowd, like the sound of the ocean or the great roar of thunder, answering, 'Alleluia! The reign of the Lord our God Almighty has begun; let us be glad and joyful and give glory to God, because this is the time for the marriage of the Lamb. His bride is ready, and she has been able to dress herself in dazzling white linen, because her linen is made of the good deeds of the saints.' The angel said, 'Write this, "Blessed are those who are invited to the wedding feast of the Lamb".'

This is the word of the Lord.

If the Responsorial Psalm is not sung the following introduction may be used:

In this Eastertime our song is Alleluia, which means Praise the Lord: we join in the praise with our response:

℟ Praise the name of the Lord.
or
℟ Alleluia!

1 Praise the Lord from the heavens,
praise him in the heights.
Praise him, all his angels,
praise him, all his host. ℟

2 Praise him, sun and moon,
praise him, shining stars.
Praise him, highest heavens
and the waters above the heavens. ℟

3 All mountains and hills,
all fruit trees and cedars,
beasts, wild and tame,
reptiles and birds on the wing. ℟

4 All earth's kings and peoples,
earth's princes and rulers:
young men and maidens,
old men together with children. ℟

Old Testament 10

Reading 10

The work style may be different but this is a reading for today's social situation. It sees a sharing in the business of marriage, an acceptance of dependence one on another. Each spouse supporting the other may be the modern way of seeing this, but living according to God's will may be the real foundation.

NRSV

A reading from the book of Proverbs *31:10-13.19-20.30-31*

A woman who fears the Lord is to be praised.

A capable wife who can find? She is far more precious than jewels. The heart of her husband trusts in her, and he will have no lack of gain. She does him good, and not harm, all the days of her life. She seeks wool and flax, and works with willing hands.

She puts her hands to the distaff, and her hands hold the spindle. She opens her hand to the poor, and reaches out her hands to the needy.

Charm is deceitful, and beauty is vain, but a woman who fears the Lord is to be praised. Give her a share in the fruit of her hands, and let her works praise her in the city gates.

This is the word of the Lord.

NJB

A reading from the book of Proverbs *31:10-13.19-20.30-31*

The woman who fears the Lord is the one to praise.

The truly capable woman – who can find her?
She is far beyond the price of pearls.
Her husband's heart has confidence in her,
from her he will derive no little profit.
Advantage and not hurt she brings him
all the days of her life.
She selects wool and flax,
she does her work with eager hands.
She sets her hands to the distaff,
her fingers grasp the spindle.
She holds out her hands to the poor,
she opens her arms to the needy.
Charm is deceitful, and beauty empty;
the woman who fears the Lord is the one to praise.
Give her a share in what her hands have worked for,
and let her works tell her praises at the city gates.

This is the word of the Lord.

If the Responsorial Psalm is not sung the following introduction may be used:

The blessings of a united family life are praised in this psalm; our response thanks God for such happiness:

℟ O blessed are those who fear the Lord!

1 O blessed are those who fear the Lord
and walk in his ways!
By the labour of your hands you shall eat.
You will be happy and prosper. ℟

2 Your wife will be like a fruitful vine
in the heart of your house;
your children like shoots of the olive,
around your table. ℟

3 Indeed thus shall be blessed
the man who fears the Lord.
May the Lord bless you from Zion
all the days of your life! ℟

NEW TESTAMENT READINGS

Reading 1

On this day of joy and celebration we are reminded by St Paul that the Cross is never very far away in the life of any Christian. The love that Christ showed was so powerful that it overcame suffering and death. In their mutual love which shares in God's love each married couple meets the problems and difficulties of life with confidence.

NRSV

A reading from the letter of St Paul to the Romans
8:31-35.37-39

Who will separate us from the love of Christ?

If God is for us, who is against us? He who did not withhold his own Son, but gave him up for all of us, will he not with him also give us everything else? Who will bring any charge against God's elect? It is God who justifies. Who is to condemn? It is Christ Jesus, who died, yes, who was raised, who is at the right hand of God, who indeed intercedes for us. Who will separate us from the love of Christ? Will hardship, or distress, or persecution, or famine, or nakedness, or peril, or sword?

No, in all these things we are more than conquerors through him who loved us. For I am convinced that neither death, nor life, nor angels, nor rulers, nor things present, nor things to come, nor powers, nor height, nor depth, nor anything else in all creation, will be able to separate us from the love of God in Christ Jesus our Lord.

This is the word of the Lord.

NJB

A reading from the letter of St Paul to the Romans

8:31-35.37-39

Nothing will be able to come between us and the love of Christ.

If God is for us, who can be against us? Since he did not spare his own Son, but gave him up for the sake of all of us, then can we not expect that with him he will freely give us all his gifts? Who can bring any accusation against those that God has chosen? When God grants saving justice who can condemn? Are we not sure that it is Christ Jesus, who died – yes and more, who was raised from the dead and is at God's right hand – and who is adding his plea for us? Can anything cut us off from the love of Christ – can hardships or distress, or persecution, or lack of food and clothing, or threats or violence? No; we come through all these things triumphantly victorious, by the power of him who loved us. For I am certain of this: neither death nor life, nor angels, nor principalities, nothing already in existence and nothing still to come, nor any power, not the heights nor the depths, nor any created thing whatever, will be able to come between us and the love of God, known to us in Christ Jesus our Lord.

This is the word of the Lord.

New Testament 2

Reading 2

This reading presents a programme for love. Married love is not selfish and closed in, but builds a community of love. Children learn how to love in that atmosphere. The whole local community benefits from such love in action.

*The reader may want to take the passage slowly, as the short sentences contain a lot of meaning. Being very familiar with the message will help in the expressing of it. (Shorter form ends at *)*

NRSV

A reading from the letter of St Paul to the Romans

12:1-2.9-18

Present your bodies as a living sacrifice, holy and acceptable to God.

I appeal to you therefore, brothers and sisters, by the mercies of God, to present your bodies as a living sacrifice, holy and acceptable to God, which is your spiritual worship. Do not be conformed to this world, but be transformed by the renewing of your minds, so that you may discern what is the will of God – what is good and acceptable and perfect.

Let love be genuine; hate what is evil, hold fast to what is good; love one another with mutual affection; outdo one another in showing honour. Do not lag in zeal, be ardent in spirit, serve the Lord. Rejoice in hope, be patient in suffering, persevere in prayer. Contribute to the needs of the saints; extend hospitality to strangers.*

Bless those who persecute you; bless and do not curse them. Rejoice with those who rejoice, weep with those who weep. Live in harmony with one another; do not be haughty, but associate with the lowly; do not claim to be wiser than you are. Do not repay anyone evil for evil, but take thought for what is noble in the sight of all. If it is possible, so far as it depends on you, live peaceably with all.

This is the word of the Lord.

NJB

A reading from the letter of St Paul to the Romans

12:1-2.9-18

Offer your bodies as a living sacrifice acceptable to God.

I urge you then, brothers, remembering the mercies of God, to offer your bodies as a living sacrifice, dedicated and acceptable to God; that is the kind of worship for you, as sensible people. Do not model your behaviour on the contemporary world, but let the renewing of your minds transform you, so that you may discern for yourselves what is the will of God – what is good and acceptable and mature.

Let love be without any pretence. Avoid what is evil; stick to what is good. In brotherly love let your feelings of deep affection for one another come to expression and regard others as more important than yourself. In the service of the Lord, work not half-heartedly but with conscientiousness and an eager spirit. Be joyful in hope, persevere in hardship; keep praying regularly; share with any of God's holy people who are in need; look for opportunities to be hospitable.*

Bless your persecutors; never curse them, bless them. Rejoice with others when they rejoice, and be sad with those in sorrow. Give the same consideration to all others alike. Pay no regard to social standing, but meet humble people on their own terms. Do not congratulate yourself on your own wisdom. Never pay back evil with evil, but bear in mind the ideals that all regard with respect. As much as is possible, and to the utmost of your ability, be at peace with everyone.

This is the word of the Lord.

New Testament 3

Reading 3

Through Baptism we have been made holy; the Holy Spirit dwells within us and operates in us. All our activities, spiritual and physical, should give glory to God. The marriage union is sanctified by the Holy Spirit; it is sacramental. Through sexual union husband and wife come to a unity in love that is faithful and exclusive.

NRSV

A reading from the first letter of St Paul to the Corinthians *6:13-15. 17-20*

Your body is a temple of the Holy Spirit.

The body is meant not for fornication but for the Lord, and the Lord for the body. And God raised the Lord and will also raise us by his power. Do you not know that your bodies are members of Christ?

But anyone united to the Lord becomes one spirit with him. Shun fornication! Every sin that a person commits is outside the body; but the fornicator sins against the body itself. Or do you not know that your body is a temple of the Holy Spirit within you, which you have from God, and that you are not your own? For you were bought with a price; therefore glorify God in your body.

This is the word of the Lord.

NJB

A reading from the first letter of St Paul to the Corinthians
6:13-15.17-20

Your body is the temple of the Holy Spirit.

The body is not for sexual immorality, it is for the Lord, and the Lord is for the body. God raised up the Lord and he will raise us up too by his power. Do you not realise that your bodies are members of Christ's body? But anyone who attaches himself to the Lord is one spirit with him.

Keep away from sexual immorality. All other sins that someone may commit are done outside the body; but the sexually immoral person sins against his own body. Do you not realise that your body is the temple of the Holy Spirit, who is in you and whom you received from God? You are not your own property, then; you have been bought at a price. So use your body for the glory of God.

This is the word of the Lord.

New Testament 4

Reading 4

This seems to be the most popular reading for weddings. It expresses what every married couple would like their love to be. St Paul certainly spells out a love that is much deeper than that sung about in the pop culture. He first of all reminds us to pray for the gift of love above all else. Again the reader must be careful not to rattle off the qualities of love, but to give the congregation time to savour and examine each quality.

NRSV

A reading from the first letter of St Paul to the Corinthians *12:31-13:8*

If I do not have love, I gain nothing.

But strive for the greater gifts. And I will show you a still more excellent way.

If I speak in the tongues of mortals and of angels, but do not have love, I am a noisy gong or a clanging cymbal. And if I have prophetic powers, and understand all mysteries and all knowledge, and if I have all faith, so as to remove mountains, but do not have love, I am nothing. If I give away all my possessions, and if I hand over my body so that I may boast, but do not have love, I gain nothing.

Love is patient; love is kind; love is not envious or boastful or arrogant or rude. It does not insist on its own way; it is not irritable or resentful; it does not rejoice in wrongdoing, but rejoices in the truth. It bears all things, believes all things, hopes all things, endures all things.

Love never ends.

This is the word of the Lord.

NJB

A reading from the first letter of St Paul to the Corinthians
12:31-13:8

If I am without love, it will do me no good whatever.

Set your mind on the higher gifts. And now I am going to put before you the best way of all.

Though I command languages both human and angelic – if I speak without love, I am no more than a gong booming or a cymbal clashing.

And though I have the power of prophecy, to penetrate all mysteries and knowledge, and though I have all the faith necessary to move mountains – if I am without love, I am nothing.

Though I should give away to the poor all that I possess, and even give up my body to be burned – if I am without love, it will do me no good whatever.

Love is always patient and kind; love is never jealous; love is not boastful or conceited, it is never rude and never seeks its own advantage, it does not take offence or store up grievances.

Love does not rejoice at wrongdoing, but finds its joy in the truth. It is always ready to make allowances, to trust, to hope and to endure whatever comes.

Love never comes to an end.

This is the word of the Lord.

Reading 5

Marriage stands as a sign of Christ's unity with the Church, his Body. As Christ loved, so each partner is called to give unselfishly to the other. (*Shorter version,* 5:2.25-32, *given here*)

NRSV

A reading from the letter of St Paul to the Ephesians

5:2. 21-33

This is a great mystery, and I am applying it to Christ and the Church.

Live in love, as Christ loved us and gave himself up for us, a fragrant offering and sacrifice to God. Husbands, love your wives, just as Christ loved the Church and gave himself up for her, in order to make her holy by cleansing her with the washing of water by the word, so as to present the Church to himself in splendour, without a spot or wrinkle or anything of the kind – yes, so that she may be holy and without blemish. In the same way, husbands should love their wives as they do their own bodies. He who loves his wife loves himself. For no one ever hates his own body, but he nourishes and tenderly cares for it, just as Christ does for the Church, because we are members of his body. 'For this reason a man will leave his father and mother and be joined to his wife, and the two will become one flesh.' This is a great mystery, and I am applying it to Christ and the Church.

This is the word of the Lord.

NJB

A reading from the letter of St Paul to the Ephesians
5:2. 21-33

Follow Christ by loving as he loved you, giving himself up for us as an offering and a sweet-smelling sacrifice to God. Husbands should love their wives, just as Christ loved the Church and sacrificed himself for her to make her holy by washing her in cleansing water with a form of words, so that when he took the Church to himself she would be glorious, with no speck or wrinkle or anything like that, but holy and faultless. In the same way, husbands must love their wives as they love their own bodies; for a man to love his wife is for him to love himself. A man never hates his own body, but he feeds it and looks after it; and that is the way Christ treats the Church, because we are parts of his Body. This is why a man leaves his father and mother and becomes attached to his wife, and the two become one flesh. This mystery has great significance, but I am applying it to Christ and the Church. To sum up: you also, each one of you, must love his wife as he loves himself; and let every wife respect her husband.

This is the word of the Lord.

Pronunciation:
EphESians

New Testament 6

Reading 6

St Paul gives here a recipe for Christian community living. He illustrates love in practice. All that any couple could hope for their life together and for their family is expressed in this reading. In particular, the need for reconciliation as soon as differences arise is stressed. The reader should easily gain the full attention of the congregation as he or she puts before them this set of ideals.

NRSV

A reading from the letter of St Paul to the Colossians
3:12-17

Above all, clothe yourselves with love, which binds everything together in perfect harmony.

As God's chosen ones, holy and beloved, clothe yourselves with compassion, kindness, humility, meekness, and patience. Bear with one another and, if anyone has a complaint against another, forgive each other; just as the Lord has forgiven you, so you also must forgive. Above all, clothe yourselves with love, which binds everything together in perfect harmony. And let the peace of Christ rule in your hearts, to which indeed you were called in the one body. And be thankful. Let the word of Christ dwell in you richly; teach and admonish one another in all wisdom; and with gratitude in your hearts sing psalms, hymns, and spiritual songs to God. And whatever you do, in word or deed, do everything in the name of the Lord Jesus, giving thanks to God the Father through him.

This is the word of the Lord.

NJB

A reading from the letter of St Paul to the Colossians
3:12-17

Over all these clothes, put on love, the perfect bond.

As the chosen people of God, then, the holy people whom he loves, you are to be clothed in heartfelt compassion, in generosity and humility, gentleness and patience. Bear with one another; forgive each other if one of you has a complaint against another. The Lord has forgiven you; now you must do the same. Over all these clothes, put on love, the perfect bond. And may the peace of Christ reign in your hearts, because it is for this that you were called together in one body. Always be thankful.

Let the Word of Christ, in all its richness, find a home with you. Teach each other, and advise each other, in all wisdom. With gratitude in your hearts sing psalms and hymns and inspired songs to God; and whatever you say or do, let it be in the name of the Lord Jesus, in thanksgiving to God the Father through him.

This is the word of the Lord.

Pronunciation:
CoLOSSians

Reading 7

It would be too easy to be put off by the first sentence. The context of the words in the period when they were written has to be taken into account. And there are different kinds of obedience. The rest of the passage talks about respect for each other, sympathy, compassion and forgiveness. This passage is not about anyone domineering over another person. It speaks more about moderation and understanding in all things. It should at least be read as a basis for discussion, for in time some agreement will have to be reached on who takes the various decisions in married life. The reader can stress the important points in the passage.

NRSV

A reading from the first letter of St Peter *3:1-9*

All of you, have unity of spirit, sympathy, love for one another.

Wives, in the same way, accept the authority of your husbands, so that, even if some of them do not obey the word, they may be won over without a word by their wives' conduct, when they see the purity and reverence of your lives. Do not adorn yourselves outwardly by braiding your hair, and by wearing gold ornaments or fine clothing; rather, let your adornment be the inner self with the lasting beauty of a gentle and quiet spirit, which is very precious in God's sight. It was in this way long ago that the holy women who hoped in God used to adorn themselves by accepting the authority of their husbands. Thus Sarah obeyed Abraham and called him lord. You have become her daughters as long as you do what is good and never let fears alarm you.

Husbands, in the same way, show consideration for your wives in your life together, paying honour to the woman as the weaker sex, since they too are also heirs of the gracious gift of life – so that nothing may hinder your prayers.

Finally, all of you, have unity of spirit, sympathy, love for one another, a tender heart, and a humble mind. Do not repay evil for evil or abuse for abuse; but, on the contrary, repay with a blessing. It is for this that you were called – that you might inherit a blessing.

This is the word of the Lord.

NJB

A reading from the first letter of St Peter *3:1-9*

You should all agree among yourselves and be sympathetic.

You wives should be obedient to your husbands. Then if there are some husbands who do not believe the Word, they may find themselves won over, without a word spoken, by the way their wives behave, when they see the reverence and purity of your way of life. Your adornment should not be an exterior one, consisting of braided hair or gold jewellery or fine clothing, but the interior disposition of the heart, consisting in the imperishable quality of a gentle and peaceful spirit, so precious in the sight of God. That was how the holy women of the past dressed themselves attractively – they hoped in God and were submissive to their husbands; like Sarah, who was obedient to Abraham, and called him her lord. You are now her children, as long as you live good lives free from fear and worry.

In the same way, husbands must always treat their wives with consideration in their life together, respecting a woman as one who, though she may be the weaker partner, is equally an heir to the generous gift of life. This will prevent anything coming in the way of your prayers.

Finally, you should all agree among yourselves and be sympathetic; love the brothers, have compassion and be self-effacing. Never repay one wrong with another, or one abusive word with another; instead, repay with a blessing. That is what you are called to do, so that you inherit a blessing.

This is the word of the Lord.

New Testament 8

Reading 8

Again, a passage that speaks about the real meaning of love. It could be another version of the cartoon, 'Love is...' Truthfulness is stressed here. That truth will lead to a good conscience. Honesty and truthfulness of the partners in marriage with each other will make their love grow on a solid foundation. And that calls for constant watchfulness and effort. The reader may have difficulty with the longer sentence construction in the letter of St John. He or she will need to become familiar with the whole thought of the sentence first, and can then phrase it bit by bit. The printed pattern of sense lines may help this.

NRSV

A reading from the first letter of St John *3:18-24*

Let us love in truth and action.

Little children, let us love, not in word or speech, but in truth and action. And by this we will know that we are from the truth and will reassure our hearts before him whenever our hearts condemn us; for God is greater than our hearts, and he knows everything. Beloved, if our hearts do not condemn us, we have boldness before God; and we receive from him whatever we ask, because we obey his commandments and do what pleases him. And this is his commandment, that we should believe in the name of his Son Jesus Christ and love one another, just as he has commanded us. All who obey his commandments abide in him, and he abides in them. And by this we know that he abides in us, by the Spirit that he has given us.

This is the word of the Lord.

NJB

A reading from the first letter of St John *3:18-24*

Our love must be something active and genuine.

Children,
our love must be not just words or mere talk,
but something active and genuine.
This will be the proof that we belong to the truth,
and it will convince us in his presence,
even if our own feelings condemn us,
that God is greater than our feelings
and knows all things.
My dear friends,
if our own feelings do not condemn us,
we can be fearless before God,
and whatever we ask
we shall receive from him,
because we keep his commandments
and do what is acceptable to him.
His commandment is this,
that we should believe in the name of his Son
Jesus Christ
and that we should love each other
as he commanded us.
Whoever keeps his commandments
remains in God, and God in him.
And this is the proof that he remains in us:
the Spirit that he has given us.

This is the word of the Lord.

New Testament 9

Reading 9

Married couples are asked here about how they see God's love in their lives. Each one's experience of God so far is important for their life together. Christians know God's love through the story of salvation in the scriptures and in the example of Christ's life. How can our love for each other reflect that and be formed by it? The love we celebrate in this wedding has a long path of growth ahead until the love of God is complete in them.

NRSV

A reading from the first letter of St John *4:7-12*

God is love.

Beloved, let us love one another, because love is from God; everyone who loves is born of God and knows God. Whoever does not love does not know God, for God is love. God's love was revealed among us in this way: God sent his only Son into the world so that we might live through him. In this is love, not that we loved God but that he loved us and sent his Son to be the atoning sacrifice for our sins. Beloved, since God loved us so much, we also ought to love one another. No one has ever seen God; if we love one another, God lives in us, and his love is perfected in us.

This is the word of the Lord.

NJB

A reading from the first letter of St John 4:7-12

God is love.

My dear friends,
let us love each other,
since love is from God
and everyone who loves is a child of God
and knows God.
Whoever fails to love does not know God
because God is love.
This is the revelation of God's love for us,
that God sent his only Son into the world
that we might have life through him.
Love consists in this:
it is not we who loved God,
but God loved us and sent his Son
to expiate our sins.
My dear friends,
if God loved us so much
we too should love each other.
No one has ever seen God,
but as long as we love each other
God remains in us
and his love comes to perfection in us.

This is the word of the Lord.

New Testament 10

Reading 10

Joy, peace and harmony are gifts to be desired in a marriage and in the family. The key to having these is in an unselfish way of life. To think of the other before myself is the challenge. The example of Christ, who did not set out to please himself, is there for our encouragement.

NRSV

A reading from the letter of St Paul to the Romans
15:1b-3a.5-7.13

May God grant you to live in harmony with one another.

We ought not to please ourselves. Each of us must please our neighbour for the good purpose of building up the neighbour. For Christ did not please himself.

May the God of steadfastness and encouragement grant you to live in harmony with one another, in accordance with Christ Jesus, so that together you may with one voice glorify the God and Father of our Lord Jesus Christ. Welcome one another, therefore, just as Christ has welcomed you, for the glory of God.

May the God of hope fill you with all joy and peace in believing, so that you may abound in hope by the power of the Holy Spirit.

This is the word of the Lord.

NJB

A reading from the letter of St Paul to the Romans

15:1b-3a.5-7.13

Give glory to God with one heart.

It is for us not to please ourselves. Each of us must consider his neighbour's good, so that we support one another. Christ did not indulge his own feelings either. Now the God of perseverance and encouragement gives you all the same purpose, following the example of Christ Jesus, so that you may together give glory to the God and Father of our Lord Jesus Christ with one heart. Accept one another, then, for the sake of God's glory, as Christ accepted you.

May the God of hope fill you with all joy and peace in your faith, so that in the power of the Holy Spirit you may be rich in hope.

This is the word of the Lord.

New Testament 11

Reading 11

Christ desired his Church to be one in love and peace. The family, as the domestic Church, should show that unity. Marriage is a high calling, and humility, gentleness and patience are the virtues needed to live it worthily. Just as the Church must be vigilant in preserving unity, so each marriage must make the effort to maintain the bond of peace.

NRSV

A reading from the letter of St Paul to the Ephesians

4:1-6

Maintain the unity of the Spirit in the bond of peace.

I, therefore, the prisoner in the Lord, beg you to lead a life worthy of the calling to which you have been called, with all humility and gentleness, with patience, bearing with one another in love, making every effort to maintain the unity of the Spirit in the bond of peace. There is one body and one Spirit, just as you were called to the one hope of your calling, one Lord, one faith, one baptism, one God and Father of all, who is above all and through all and in all.

This is the word of the Lord.

NJB

A reading from the letter of St Paul to the Ephesians

4:1-6

Preserve the unity of the Spirit by the peace that binds you together.

I, the prisoner of the Lord, urge you therefore to lead a life worthy of the vocation to which you were called. With all humility and gentleness, and with patience, support each other in love. Take every care to preserve the unity of the Spirit by the peace that binds you together. There is one Body, one Spirit, just as one hope is the goal of your calling by God. There is one Lord, one faith, one baptism, and one God and Father of all, over all, through all and within all.

This is the word of the Lord.

New Testament 12

Reading 12

In marriage, as in the Christian life as a whole, only the highest standards should be aimed at. Peace in the family will come through that search for excellence. It is a high aim to ask any family not to worry, but it is important to recognise the lack of faith and trust in God, which is to be seen in giving way to undue anxiety. The sacrament of marriage is a promise that in all needs the Lord is near.

NRSV

A reading from the letter of St Paul to the Philippians

4:4-9

The peace of God, which surpasses all understanding, will guard your hearts.

Rejoice in the Lord always; again I will say, Rejoice. Let your gentleness be known to everyone. The Lord is near. Do not worry about anything, but in everything by prayer and supplication with thanksgiving let your requests be made known to God. And the peace of God, which surpasses all understanding, will guard your hearts and your minds in Christ Jesus. Finally, beloved, whatever is true, whatever is honourable, whatever is just, whatever is pure, whatever is pleasing, whatever is commendable, if there is any excellence and if there is anything worthy of praise, think about these things. Keep on doing the things that you have learned and received and heard and seen in me, and the God of peace will be with you.

This is the word of the Lord.

NJB

A reading from the letter of St Paul to the Philippians
4:4-9

The peace of God which is beyond our understanding will guard your hearts.

Always be joyful, then, in the Lord; I repeat, be joyful. Let your good sense be obvious to everybody. The Lord is near. Never worry about anything; but tell God all your desires of every kind in prayer and petition shot through with gratitude, and the peace of God which is beyond our understanding will guard your hearts and your thoughts in Christ Jesus. Finally, brothers, let your minds be filled with everything that is true, everything that is honourable, everything that is upright and pure, everything that we love and admire – with whatever is good and praiseworthy. Keep doing everything you learnt from me and were told by me and have heard or seen me doing. Then the God of peace will be with you.

This is the word of the Lord.

New Testament 13

Reading 13

Any couple entering marriage will have many fears and concerns about the future. This reading encourages confidence. It is a confidence coming from God's loving presence in every marriage, and from the mutual love of the couple. This love will make them hospitable, concerned and contented.

NRSV

A reading from the letter to the Hebrews *13:1-4a.5-6b*

Let marriage be held in honour by all.

Let mutual love continue. Do not neglect to show hospitality to strangers, for by doing that some have entertained angels without knowing it. Remember those who are in prison, as though you were in prison with them; those who are being tortured, as though you yourselves were being tortured. Let marriage be held in honour by all. Keep your lives free from the love of money, and be content with what you have; for he has said, 'I will never leave you or forsake you.' So we can say with confidence, 'The Lord is my helper; I will not be afraid.'

This is the word of the Lord.

NJB

A reading from the letter to the Hebrews *13:1-4a.5-6b*

Marriage must be honoured by all.

Continue to love each other like brothers, and remember always to welcome strangers, for by doing this, some people have entertained angels without knowing it. Keep in mind those who are in prison, as though you were in prison with them; and those who are being badly treated, since you too are in the body. Marriage must be honoured by all. Put avarice out of your lives and be content with whatever you have; God himself has said: I shall not fail you or desert you, and so we can say with confidence: With the Lord on my side, I fear nothing.

This is the word of the Lord.

GOSPEL READINGS

Reading 1

The wishes and prayers for the couple on their wedding day will be for their happiness in their new state of life. In this Gospel passage Jesus gives the recipe for happiness. It echoes the marriage vows in that it sees life made up of joys and sorrows, of challenges and struggles, and it points towards the reward of heaven beyond the parting of death.

Acclamation *1 Jn 4:8.11*

Alleluia, alleluia
God is love;
let us love one another
as God has loved us.
Alleluia!

NRSV

A reading from the holy Gospel according to Matthew *5:1-12*

Rejoice and be glad, for your reward is great in heaven.

When Jesus saw the crowds, he went up the mountain; and after he sat down, his disciples came to him. Then he began to speak, and taught them, saying:
'Blessed are the poor in spirit, for theirs is the kingdom of heaven.
'Blessed are those who mourn, for they will be comforted.
'Blessed are the meek, for they will inherit the earth.
'Blessed are those who hunger and thirst for righteousness, for they will be filled.
'Blessed are the merciful, for they will receive mercy.
'Blessed are the pure in heart, for they will see God.
'Blessed are the peacemakers, for they will be called children of God.

'Blessed are those who are persecuted for righteousness' sake, for theirs is the kingdom of heaven.
'Blessed are you when people revile you and persecute you and utter all kinds of evil against you falsely on my account.
'Rejoice and be glad, for your reward is great in heaven.'

This is the Gospel of the Lord.

NJB

A reading from the holy Gospel according to Matthew *5:1-12*

Rejoice and be glad, for your reward will be great in heaven.

Seeing the crowds, Jesus went onto the mountain. And when he was seated his disciples came to him. Then he began to speak. This is what he taught them:

How blessed are the poor in spirit:
the kingdom of Heaven is theirs.
Blessed are the gentle:
they shall have the earth as inheritance.
Blessed are those who mourn:
they shall be comforted.
Blessed are those who hunger and thirst for uprightness:
they shall have their fill.
Blessed are the merciful:
they shall have mercy shown them.
Blessed are the pure in heart:
they shall see God.
Blessed are the peacemakers:
they shall be recognised as children of God.
Blessed are those who are persecuted in the cause of uprightness:
the kingdom of Heaven is theirs.

Blessed are you when people abuse you and persecute you and speak all kinds of calumny against you falsely on my account. Rejoice and be glad, for your reward will be great in heaven.
This is the Gospel of the Lord.

Gospel 2 *Reading 2*

The freshness of relationship on a wedding day will not last, but love can grow and deepen. We hope that the marriage will not lose its taste. The public witness given by the wedding is to be seen daily in the marriage and its growth. Christian marriage can be a beacon of hope to the world.

Acclamation *1 Jn 4:12*

Alleluia alleluia!
As long as we love one another
God will live in us,
and his love will be complete in us.
Alleluia!

NRSV

A reading from the holy Gospel according to Matthew *5:13-16*

You are the light of the world.

Jesus said to his disciples, 'You are the salt of the earth; but if salt has lost its taste, how can its saltiness be restored? It is no longer good for anything, but is thrown out and trampled under foot. You are the light of the world. A city built on a hill cannot be hid. No one after lighting a lamp puts it under the bushel basket, but on the lamp stand, and it gives light to all in the house. In the same way, let your light shine before others, so that they may see your good works and give glory to your Father in heaven.'

This is the Gospel of the Lord.

NJB

A reading from the holy Gospel according to Matthew
5:13-16

You are light for the world.

Jesus said to his disciples, 'You are salt for the earth. But if salt loses its taste, what can make it salty again? It is good for nothing, and can only be thrown out to be trampled under people's feet.

'You are light for the world. A city built on a hill-top cannot be hidden. No one lights a lamp to put it under a tub; they put it on the lamp stand where it shines for everyone in the house. In the same way your light must shine in people's sight, so that, seeing your good works, they may give praise to your Father in heaven.'

This is the Gospel of the Lord.

Gospel 3 *Reading 3*

*Preparing for marriage ensures a sound foundation to the shared life. So also the first years together strengthen that foundation. The winds and storms of life will come in different forms, but if the marriage has been built solidly it will withstand all difficulty. (Shorter form ends at *)*

Acclamation *1 Jn 4:16*

Alleluia, alleluia!
Anyone who lives in love
lives in God,
and God lives in him.
Alleluia!

NRSV

A reading from the holy Gospel according to Matthew *7:21.24-29*

He built his house on rock.

Jesus said to his disciples, 'Not everyone who says to me, "Lord, Lord," will enter the kingdom of heaven, but only the one who does the will of my Father in heaven.

'Everyone then who hears these words of mine and acts on them will be like a wise man who built his house on rock. The rain fell, the floods came, and the winds blew and beat on that house, but it did not fall, because it had been founded on rock.*

And everyone who hears these words of mine and does not act on them will be like a foolish man who built his house on sand. The rain fell, and the floods came, and the winds blew and beat against that house, and it fell – and great was its fall!'

Now when Jesus had finished saying these things, the crowds were astounded at his teaching, for he taught them as one having authority, and not as their scribes.

This is the Gospel of the Lord.

NJB

A reading from the holy Gospel according to Matthew
7:21.24-29

He built his house on rock.

Jesus said to his disciples, 'It is not anyone who says to me, "Lord, Lord," who will enter the kingdom of heaven, but the person who does the will of my Father in heaven.

'Therefore, everyone who listens to these words of mine and acts on them will be like a sensible man who built his house on rock. Rain came down, floods rose, gales blew and hurled themselves against that house, and it did not fall: it was founded on rock. But everyone who listens to these words of mine and does not act on them will be like a stupid man who built his house on sand. Rain came down, floods rose, gales blew and struck that house, and it fell; and what a fall it had!'

Jesus had now finished what he wanted to say, and his teaching made a deep impression on the people because he taught them with authority, unlike their own scribes.

This is the Gospel of the Lord.

Gospel 4 *Reading 4*

A man and woman deeply in love will not hesitate on their wedding day to give themselves to each other for life. This reading recognises that God who has brought them together will be with them to keep them as one all the days of their lives.

Acclamation *1 Jn 4:7*

Alleluia, alleluia!
Everyone who loves
is begotten by God,
and knows God.
Alleluia!

NRSV

A reading from the holy Gospel according to Matthew *19:3-6*

What God has joined together, let no one separate.

Some Pharisees came to Jesus, and to test him they asked, 'Is it lawful for a man to divorce his wife for any cause?' He answered, 'Have you not read that the one who made them at the beginning "made them male and female," and said, "For this reason a man shall leave his father and mother and be joined to his wife, and the two shall become one flesh"? So they are no longer two, but one flesh. Therefore what God has joined together, let no one separate.'

This is the Gospel of the Lord.

NJB

A reading from the holy Gospel according to Matthew
19:3-6

What God has united, human beings must not divide.

Some Pharisees approached Jesus, and to put him to the test they said, 'Is it against the Law for a man to divorce his wife on any pretext whatever?' He answered, 'Have you not read that the Creator from the beginning made them male and female and that he said: This is why a man leaves his father and mother and becomes attached to his wife, and the two become one flesh? They are no longer two, therefore, but one flesh. So then, what God has united, human beings must not divide.'

This is the Gospel of the Lord.

Gospel 5

Reading 5

Love is unselfish. Being married means learning to love unselfishly. It takes courage and character to do so. It is a learning process that will take time. But love is a gift, given in freedom.

Acclamation *1 Jn 4:8.11*

Alleluia, alleluia!
God is love; let us love one another
as God has loved us.
Alleluia!

NRSV

A reading from the holy Gospel according to Matthew *22:35-40*

This is the greatest and first commandment. And a second is like it.

A lawyer asked Jesus a question to test him. 'Teacher, which commandment in the law is the greatest?' He said to him, '"You shall love the Lord your God with all your heart, and with all your soul, and with all your mind." This is the greatest and first commandment. And a second is like it: "You shall love your neighbour as yourself." On these two commandments hang all the law and the prophets.'

This is the Gospel of the Lord.

NJB

A reading from the holy Gospel according to Matthew
22:35-40

This is the greatest and the first commandment. The second resembles it.

A lawyer, to put Jesus to the test, put him a question, 'Master, which is the greatest commandment of the Law?' Jesus said to him, '"You must love the Lord your God with all your heart, with all your soul, and with all your mind." This is the greatest and the first commandment. The second resembles it: "You must love your neighbour as yourself." On these two commandments hang the whole Law, and the Prophets too.'

This is the Gospel of the Lord.

Gospel 6 *Reading 6*

People don't take easily to change. To leave home and parents is a difficult step. A man and a woman can face this break and change in life because they are so deeply in love. Going forward in real unity is the next task; there is always the danger of looking back when that task gets difficult.

Acclamation *1 Jn 4:7*

Alleluia, alleluia!
Everyone who loves
is begotten by God,
and knows God.
Alleluia!

NRSV

A reading from the holy Gospel according to Mark *10:6-9*

They are no longer two, but one flesh.

Jesus said, 'From the beginning of creation, "God made them male and female." "For this reason a man shall leave his father and mother and be joined to his wife, and the two shall become one flesh." So they are no longer two, but one flesh. Therefore what God has joined together, let no one separate.'

This is the Gospel of the Lord.

NJB

A reading from the holy Gospel according to Mark

10:6-9

They are no longer two, but one flesh.

Jesus said, 'From the beginning of creation God made them male and female. This is why a man leaves his father and mother, and the two become one flesh. They are no longer two, therefore, but one flesh. So then, what God has united, human beings must not divide.'

This is the Gospel of the Lord.

Gospel 7 *Reading 7*

Christians make Jesus and his friends welcome at their wedding. Their prayer will be that he will stay with their marriage. They trust in his power, so that if they do whatever he asks he will in their need bring forth the best wine yet.

Acclamation *1 Jn 4:12*

Alleluia, alleluia!
As long as we love one another
God will live in us,
and his love will be complete in us.
Alleluia!

NRSV

A reading from the holy Gospel according to John *2:1-11*

Jesus did this, the first of his signs, in Cana of Galilee.

There was a wedding in Cana of Galilee, and the mother of Jesus was there. Jesus and his disciples had also been invited to the wedding. When the wine gave out, the mother of Jesus said to him, 'They have no wine.' And Jesus said to her, 'Woman, what concern is that to you and to me? My hour has not yet come.' His mother said to the servants, 'Do whatever he tells you.' Now standing there were six stone water jars for the Jewish rites of purification, each holding twenty or thirty gallons. Jesus said to them, 'Fill the jars with water.' And they filled them up to the brim. He said to them, 'Now draw some out, and take it to the chief steward.' So they took it. When the steward tasted the water that had become wine, and did not know where it came from (though the servants who had drawn the water knew), the steward called the bridegroom and said to him, 'Everyone serves the good wine first, and then the inferior wine after the guests have become drunk. But you have kept the good wine until now.' Jesus did this, the first of his signs, in Cana of Galilee, and revealed his glory; and his disciples believed in him.

This is the Gospel of the Lord.

NJB

A reading from the holy Gospel according to John *2:1-11*

This was the first of Jesus' signs: it was at Cana in Galilee.

There was a wedding at Cana in Galilee. The mother of Jesus was there, and Jesus and his disciples had also been invited. And they ran out of wine, since the wine provided for the feast had all been used, and the mother of Jesus said to him, 'they have no wine'. Jesus said, 'Woman, what do you want from me? My hour has not come yet.' His mother said to the servants, 'Do whatever he tells you.' There were six stone water jars standing there, meant for the ablutions that are customary among the Jews: each could hold twenty or thirty gallons. Jesus said to the servants, 'Fill the jars with water,' and they filled them to the brim. Then he said to them, 'draw some out now and take it to the president of the feast.' They did this; the president tasted the water, and it had turned into wine. Having no idea where it had come from – though the servants who had drawn the water knew – the president of the feast called the bridegroom and said, 'Everyone serves good wine first and the worse wine when the guests are well wined; but you have kept the best wine till now.' This was the first of Jesus' signs: it was at Cana in Galilee. He revealed his glory, and his disciples believed in him.

This is the Gospel of the Lord.

Gospel 8 *Reading 8*

Joy is the fruit of love. Jesus prays for that joy in the shared love of husband and wife. Real love is a reflection of God's love. Faithfulness to him will enable that love to abide.

Acclamation *1 Jn 4:16*

Alleluia, alleluia!
Anyone who lives in love
lives in God,
and God lives in him.
Alleluia!

NRSV

A reading from the holy Gospel according to John *15:9-12*

Abide in my love.

Jesus said to his disciples, 'As the Father has loved me, so I have loved you; abide in my love. If you keep my commandments, you will abide in my love, just as I have kept my Father's commandments and abide in his love. I have said these things to you so that my joy may be in you, and that your joy may be complete. This is my commandment, that you love one another as I have loved you.'

This is the Gospel of the Lord.

NJB

A reading from the holy Gospel according to John *15:9-12*

Remain in my love.

Jesus said to his disciples,
'I have loved you
just as the Father has loved me.
Remain in my love.
If you keep my commandments
you will remain in my love.
I have told you this
so that my own joy may be in you
and your joy be complete.
This is my commandment:
love one another,
as I have loved you.'

This is the Gospel of the Lord.

Gospel 9

Reading 9

Marriages are made in heaven, they say. Jesus says that he has called each of us to our vocation in life. He has brought together husband and wife to a life of fruitful love. He asks for faithfulness. He promises to answer their prayers in time of need.

Acclamation *1 Jn 4:8.11*

Alleluia, alleluia!
God is love;
let us love one another
as God has loved us.
Alleluia!

NRSV

A reading from the holy Gospel according to John *15:12-16*

This is my commandment, that you love one another.

Jesus said to his disciples, 'This is my commandment, that you love one another as I have loved you. No one has greater love than this, to lay down one's life for one's friends. You are my friends if you do what I command you. I do not call you servants any longer, because the servant does not know what the master is doing; but I have called you friends, because I have made known to you everything that I have heard from my Father. You did not choose me but I chose you. And I appointed you to go and bear fruit, fruit that will last, so that the Father will give you whatever you ask him in my name.'

This is the Gospel of the Lord.

NJB

A reading from the holy Gospel according to John
15:12-16

This is my commandment: love one another.

Jesus said to his disciples,
'This is my commandment:
love one another,
as I have loved you.
No one can have greater love
than to lay down his life for his friends.
You are my friends
if you do what I command you.
I shall no longer call you servants,
because a servant does not know
his master's business;
I call you friends,
because I have made known to you
everything I have learnt from my Father.
You did not choose me,
no, I chose you;
and I commissioned you
to go out and to bear fruit, fruit that will last;
so that the Father will give you
anything you ask him in my name.'

This is the Gospel of the Lord

Gospel 10 *Reading 10*

*Jesus prays for unity, he prays for this couple that they may grow towards each other and not apart from each other. He prays that their love may be as strong and enduring as his love for the Father. The Christian community at this wedding make that prayer of Jesus their own. (Shorter version ends at *)*

Acclamation *1 Jn 4:12*

Alleluia, alleluia!
As long as we love one another
God will live in us,
and his love will be complete in us.
Alleluia!

NRSV

A reading from the holy Gospel according to John *17:20-26*

That they may become completely one.

Jesus lifted up his eyes to heaven, and said, 'Holy Father, I ask not only on behalf of these, but also on behalf of those who will believe in me through their word, that they may all be one. As you, Father, are in me and I am in you, may they also be in us, so that the world may believe that you have sent me. The glory that you have given me I have given them, so that they may be one, as we are one, I in them and you in me, that they may become completely one, so that the world may know that you have sent me and have loved them even as you have loved me. *

Father, I desire that those also, whom you have given me, may be with me where I am, to see my glory, which you have given me because you loved me before the foundation of the world. 'Righteous Father, the world does not know you, but I know you; and these know that you have sent me. I made your name known to them, and I will make it known, so that the love with which you have loved me may be in them, and I in them.'

This is the Gospel of the Lord.

NJB

Gospel 10

A reading from the holy Gospel according to John
17:20-26

That they may they be perfected in unity.

Jesus raised his eyes to heaven, and said:
'Father,
I pray not only for these
but also for those
who through their teaching will come to believe in me.
May they all be one,
just as, Father, you are in me and I am in you,
so that they also may be in us,
so that the world may believe it was you who sent me.
I have given them the glory you gave to me,
that they may be one as we are one.
With me in them and you in me,
may they be so perfected in unity
that the world will recognise that it was you who sent me
and that you loved them as you loved me.*
Father,
I want those you have given me
to be with me where I am,
so that they may always see my glory
which you have given me
because you loved me
before the foundation of the world.
Father, Upright One,
the world has not known you,
but I have known you,
and these have known
that you have sent me.
I have made your name known to them
and will continue to make it known,
so that the love with which you loved me may be in them,
and so that I may be in them.

This is the Gospel of the Lord.